First published in the UK in 2006
by Bailey Hart Publishing
8 Oman Avenue
London NW2 6BG

www.baileyhartpublishing.com

10 9 8 7 6 5 4 3 2 1

ISBN 0-9552843-0-9
978-0-9552843-0-4

Text compilation and Photography by Richard Bailey.
Design and Typography by Hun Wynn
Printed by Toppan Printing Ltd

bhp bailey hart publishing

" TO BE A DAD "

**BABIES**

"

ARE SUCH A NICE WAY TO START PEOPLE.

"

DON HEROLD

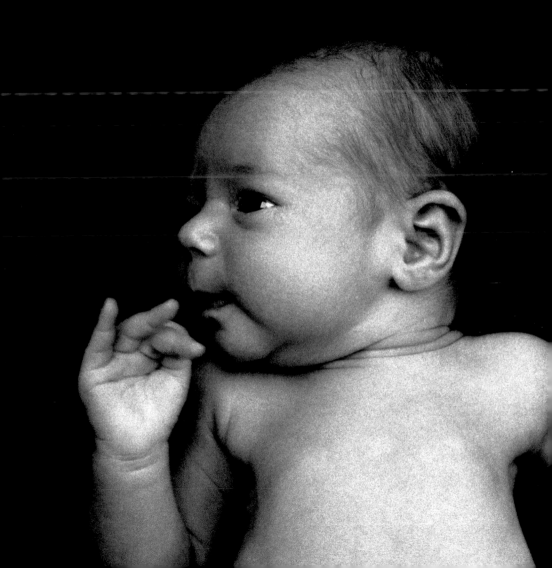

**"** NO
BABY
IS
ADMIRED
SUFFICIENTLY
TO
PLEASE
THE
PARENTS
**"**

DAVE BERNARD

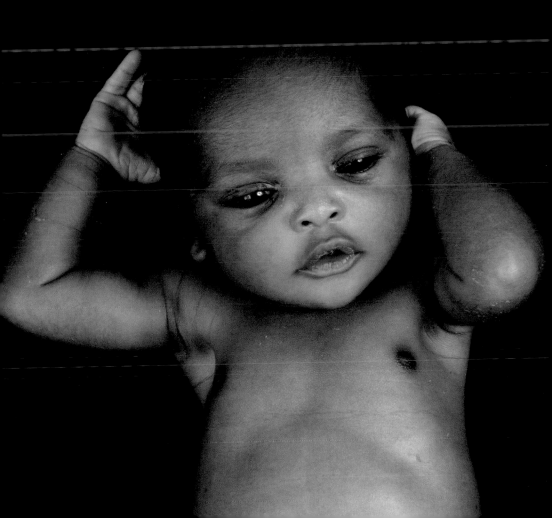

THE QUICKEST WAY
FOR A
PARENT
TO GET
A CHILD'S ATTENTION
IS TO SIT DOWN
AND LOOK
COMFORTABLE
"

LANE OLINGHOUSE

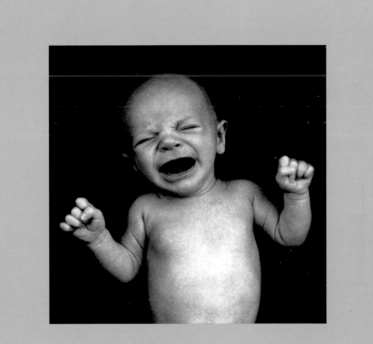

A BABY WILL MAKE LOVE STRONGER,

DAYS SHORTER, NIGHT LONGER,

BANKROLL SMALLER,

HOME HAPPIER,

CLOTHES SHABBIER,

THE PAST FORGOTTEN

&

THE FUTURE WORTH LIVING FOR.

ANON

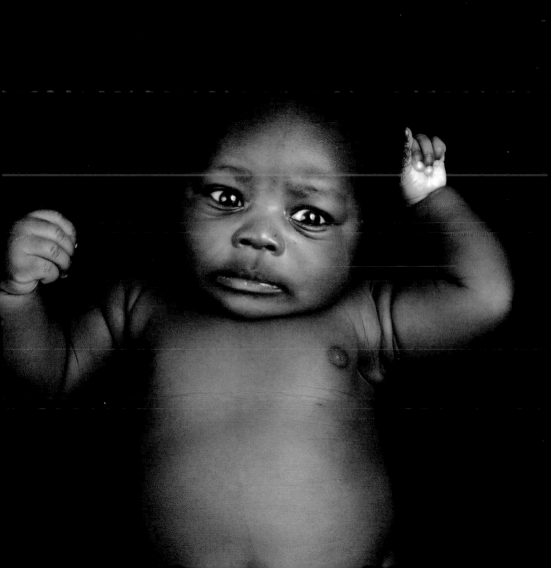

"

THIS IS THE BASIC BABY MOOD CYCLE,

WHICH ALL BABIES SETTLE INTO

ONCE THEY GET OVER BEING BORN:

MOOD **1** JUST ABOUT TO CRY.

MOOD **2** CRYING.

MOOD **3** JUST FINISHED CRYING

"

ANON

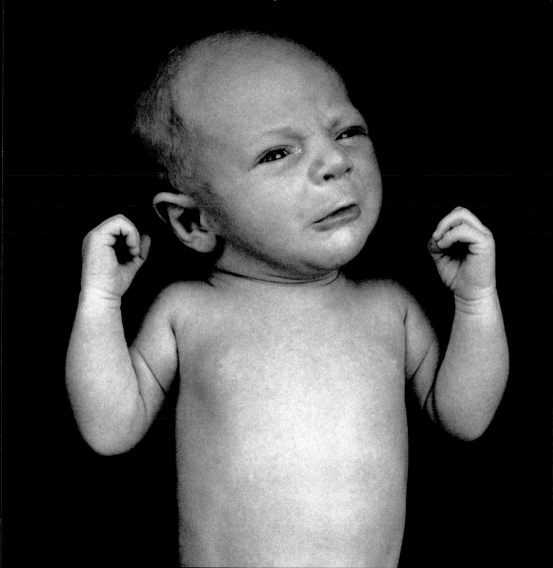

 I LIKE CHILDREN.

PROPERLY "

W.C. FIELDS

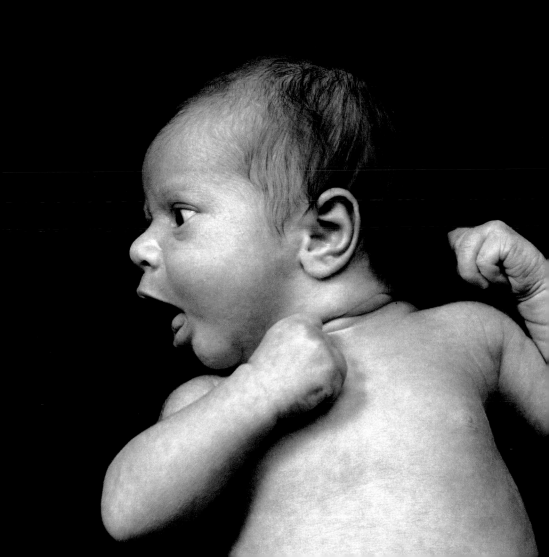

" I THINK GOD
**MADE BABIES CUTE**

**SO WE DON'T EAT THEM.**
ROBIN WILLIAMS

"

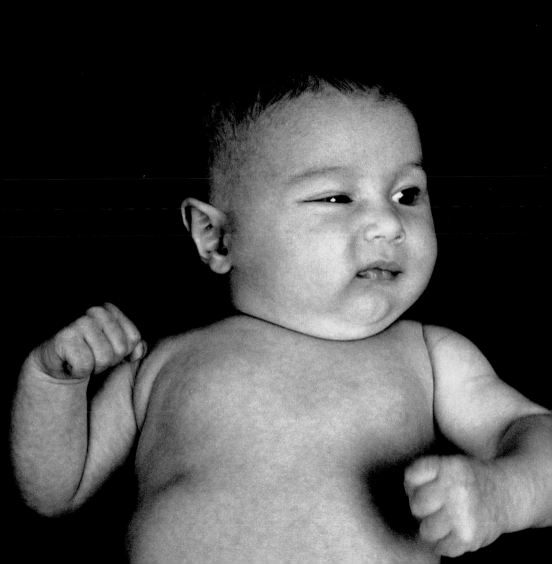

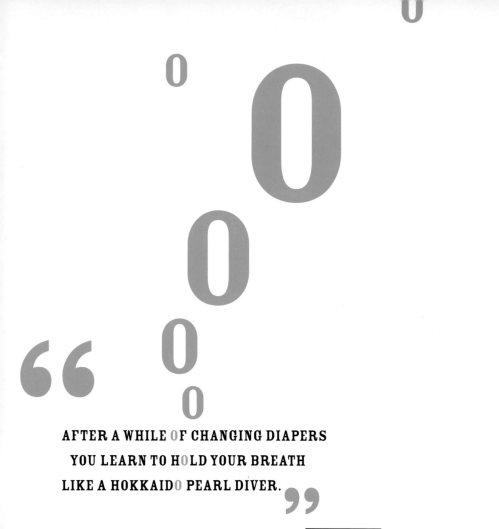

" AFTER A WHILE OF CHANGING DIAPERS
YOU LEARN TO HOLD YOUR BREATH
LIKE A HOKKAIDO PEARL DIVER. "

**DENNIS MILLER**

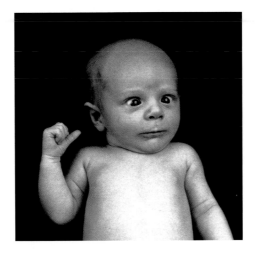

**" FOR A FATHER,**
**A HOME BIRTH IS PREFERABLE.**
**THAT WAY**

**YOU'RE NOT MISSING ANYTHING ON  TELEVISION. "**

JEREMY HARDY

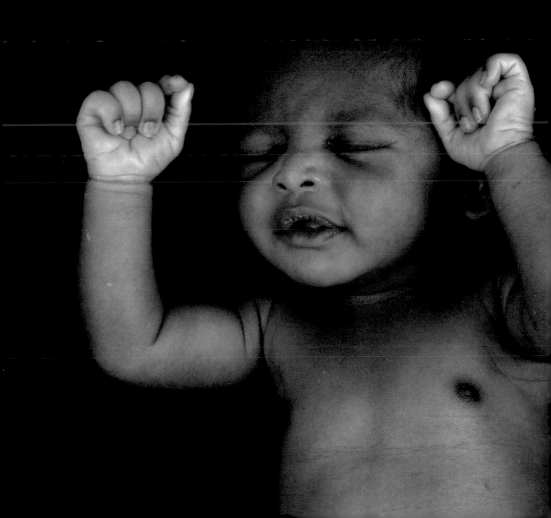

 **YEAH,**

SURE,

FOR YOU,

A BABIES ALL FUN AND GAMES.

FOR ME ITS DIAPER CHANGES

AND MIDNIGHT FEEDINGS...

### Doesn't mum do all that stuff?

 **YEAH,**

BUT I HAVE TO HEAR ABOUT IT.

`HOMER SIMPSON`

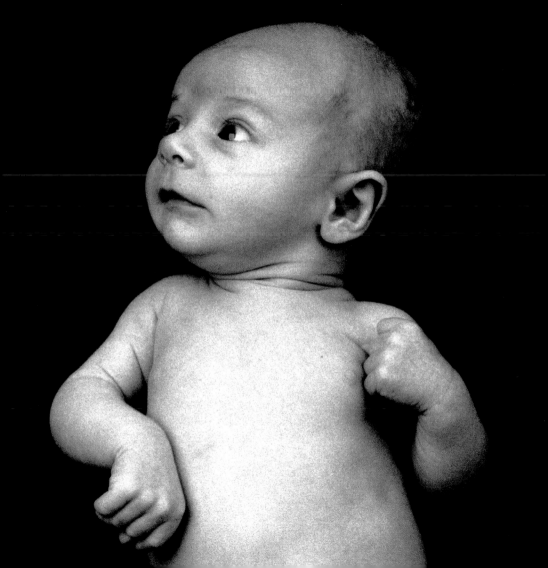

" CHILDREN ARE THE ONLY FORM OF **immortality** THAT WE CAN BE SURE OF "

PETER USTINOV

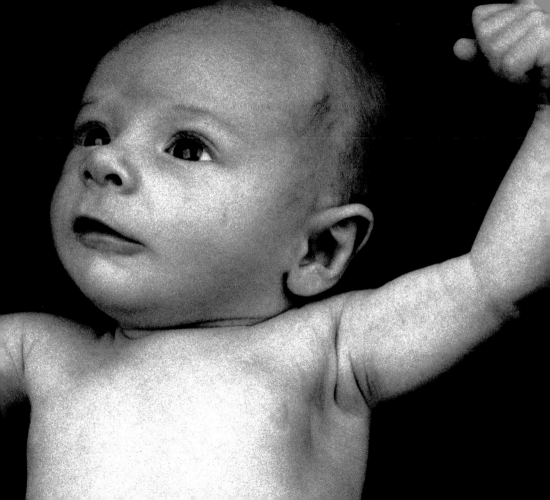

A DAD IS THE ONE WHO GETS YOUR

## maths homework

WRONG.

JANE, AGED 8

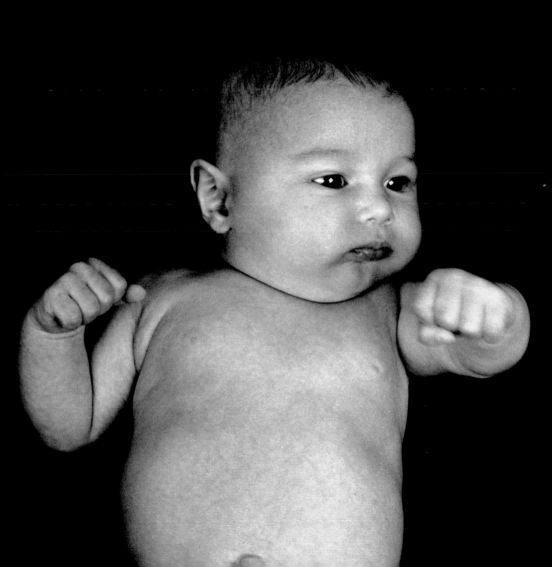

 IF MEN HAD TO HAVE BABIES,

THEY WOULD ONLY EVER HAVE

**EACH.**

**PRINCESS DIANA**

" KIDS.

THEY'RE NOT EASY. BUT THERE HAS TO BE SOME PENALTY FOR SE

BILL MAHER

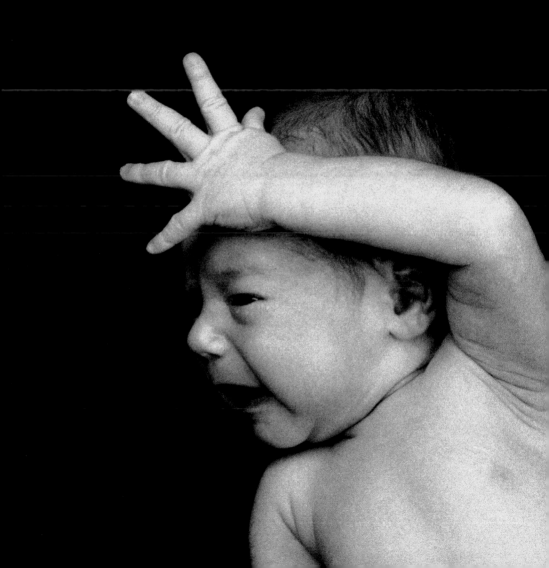

**❝**

MY NEW SON HAS A FACE LIKE THAT OF AN AGEING RAILWAY PORTER

WHO IS BEGINNING TO REALIZE THAT HIS UNTIDINESS

HAS MEANT THAT HE'LL NEVER GET THAT TICKET COLLECTORS JOB

HE'S BEEN AFTER FOR TWENTY YEARS. **❞**

KINGSLEY AMIS

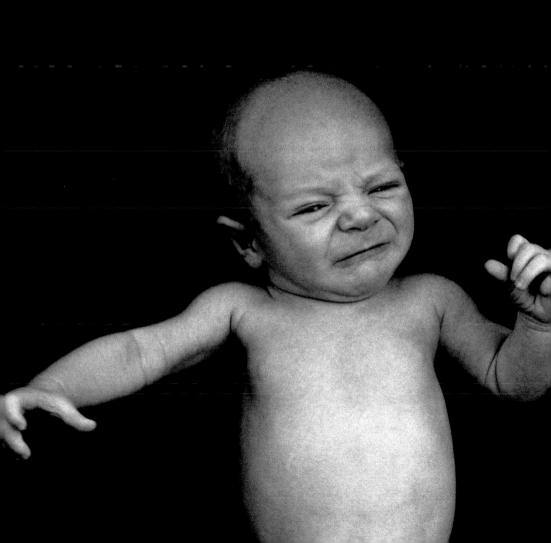

**"THE TOUGHEST PART OF PARENTHOOD HAS NOTHING TO DO WITH**

PUTTING FOOD ON THE TABLE,

CLOTHES IN THE CLOSET,

OR

TUITION MONEY IN THE BANK.

**THE TOUGHEST PART OF PARENTHOOD**

IS NEVER KNOWING IF YOU'RE DOING THE RIGHT THING. **"**

D.L. STEWART

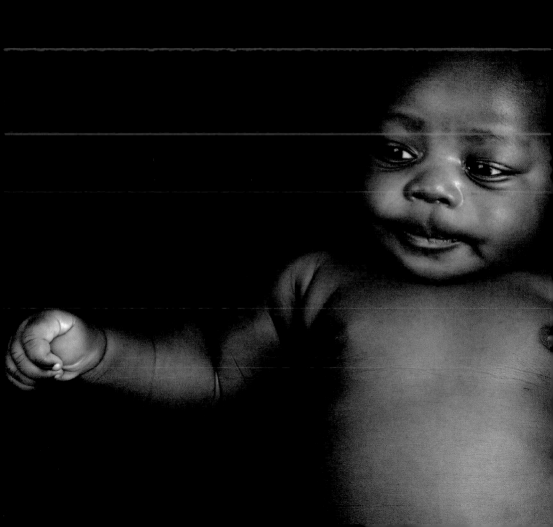

"

# CHILDREN NEED LOVE,

## ESPECIALLY WHEN THEY DO NOT DESERVE IT

"

ANON

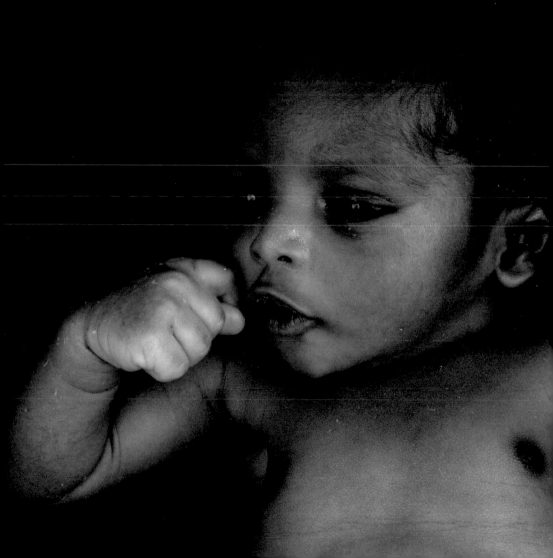

**FOR MEN,**

**CHILDBIRTH IS THAT CRUELLEST OF COMBINATIONS:**

STRESSFUL

AND boring

"

MARCUS BERKMANN

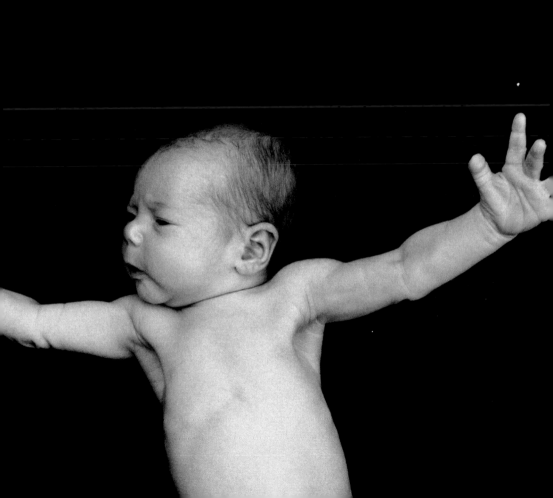

**I WAS SO**

# UGLY

**AT BIRTH**

THAT THE MIDWIFE TOOK ONE LOOK AT ME

TURNED

AND SLAPPED

MY FATHER.

JOAN RIVERS

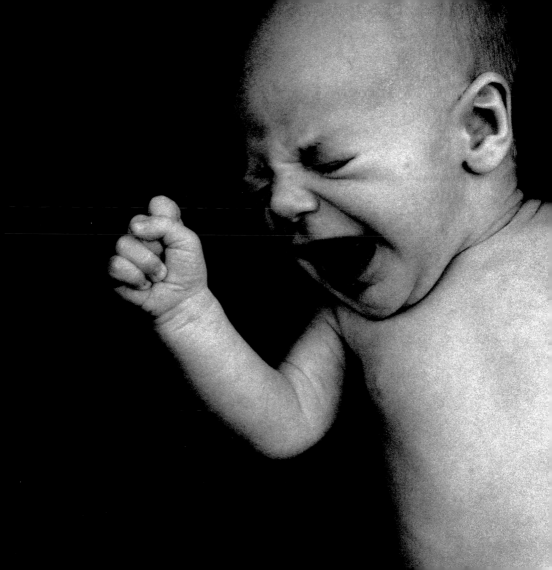

## FOR SALE:

1993 TOYATA SUPRA TWIN TURBO,
£14,250, VERY RARE, EVERY TOY,
TRACTION, CRUISE, PRIVATE NUMBER PLATE,
160 MPH, AWESOME,
GIRLFRIEND FORGOT TO TAKE PILL, GUTTED.

ADVERT IN AUTOTRADER MAGAZINE

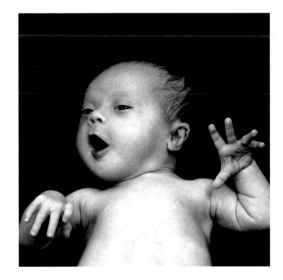

**66**

MY FATHER GAVE ME THE GREATEST GIFT ANYONE COULD GIVE ANOTHER PERSON:

HE BELIEVED IN ME.

**99**

JIM VALVANO

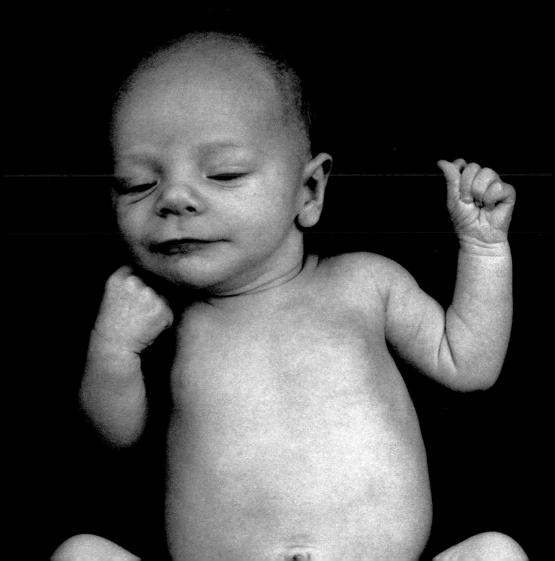

**"**

REMEMBER THAT CHILDREN,

MARRIAGES

AND

FLOWER GARDENS

REFLECT
THE
KIND OF CARE
THEY GET.

**"**

H.JACKSON BROWN JR

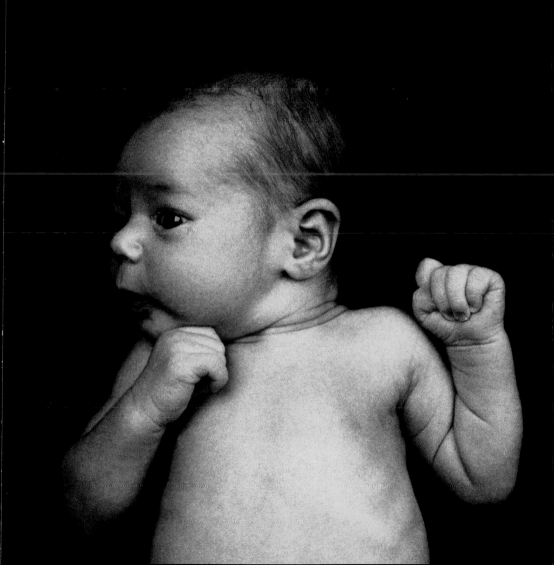

**"** WHILE WE TRY TO TEACH OUR CHILDREN ALL ABOUT LIFE,

OUR CHILDREN TEACH US WHAT LIFE IS ALL ABOUT.

**"**

ANON

**"** WHEN YOU'RE DRAWING UP YOUR LIST OF LIFE'S MIRACLES,
YOU MIGHT PLACE NEAR THE TOP

THE FIRST MOMENT YOUR BABY SMILES AT YOU.

**"**

BOB GREENE

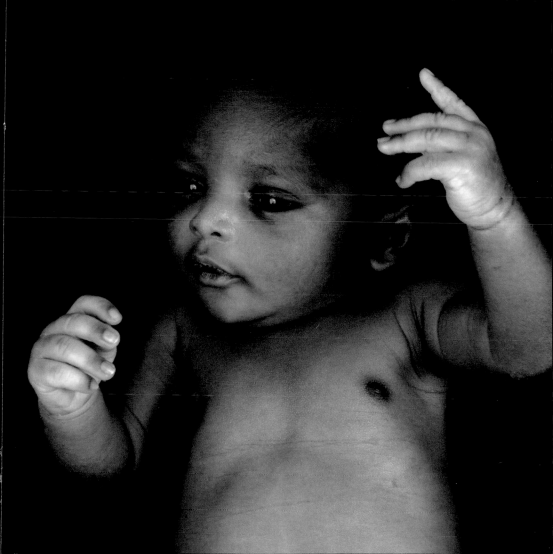

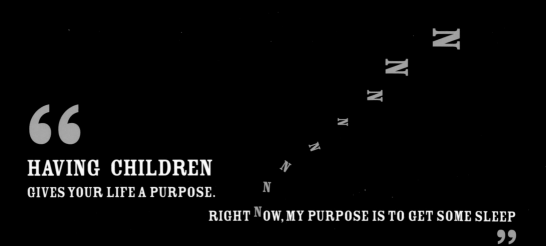

**"**

## HAVING  CHILDREN

### GIVES YOUR LIFE A PURPOSE.

### RIGHT NOW, MY PURPOSE IS TO GET SOME SLEEP

**"**

RENO GOODALE

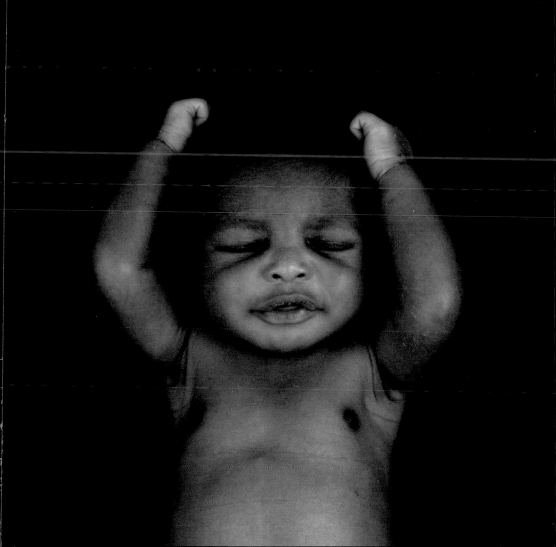

"

A FATHER
IS SOMEONE
WHO CARRIES
PICTURES
WHERE
HIS MONEY
USED TO BE

"

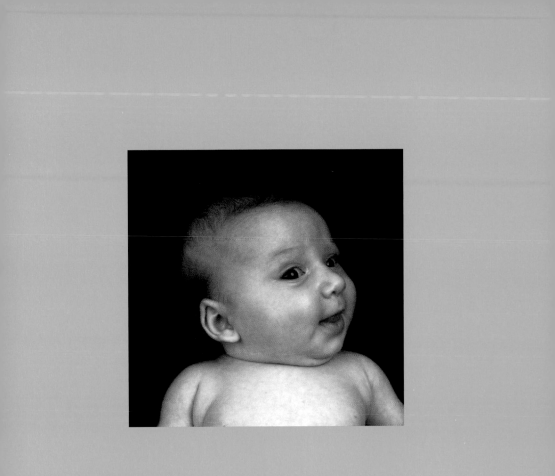

"WHEN THE FIRST BABY LAUGHED FOR THE FIRST TIME,

THE LAUGH BROKE INTO A THOUSAND PIECES

AND THEY ALL WENT SKIPPING ABOUT

AND THAT WAS THE BEGINNING OF FAIRIES."

SIR JAMES BARRIE IN PETER PAN

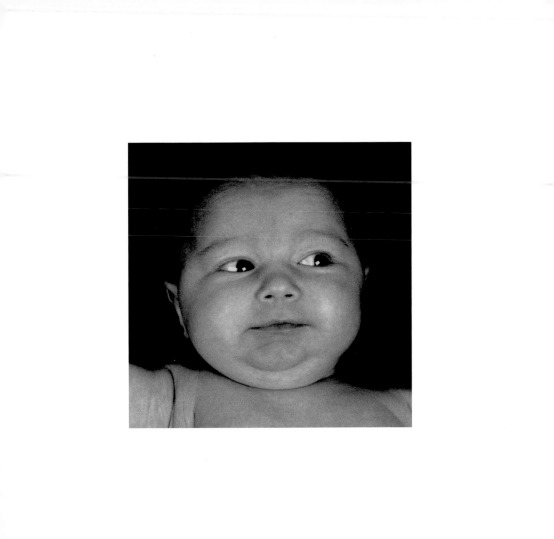

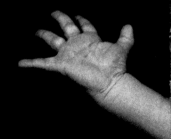

"

HAVING A BABY CHANGES THE WAY YOU VIEW YOUR IN-LAWS.
I LOVE IT WHEN THEY COME TO VISIT NOW.

THEY CAN HOLD THE BABY AND I CAN GO OUT.

"

MATTHEW BRODERICK

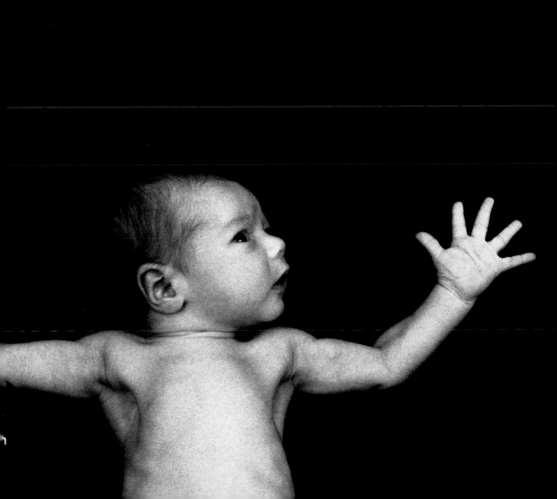

ANY MAN CAN BECOME A FATHER.

IT TAKES SOMEONE SPECIAL TO BE A DAD.

**ANON**

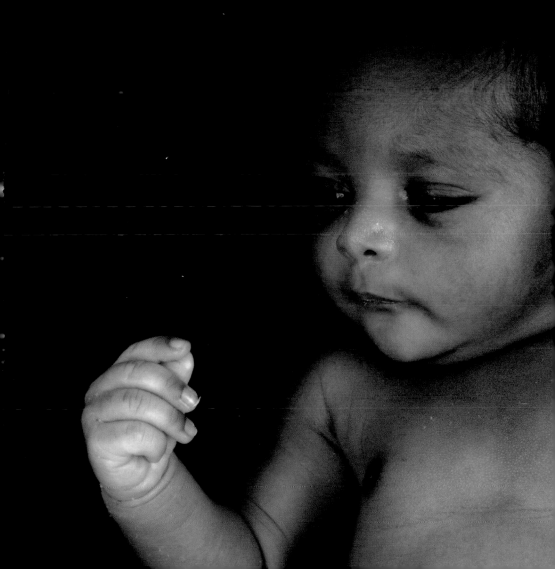

**RAISING KIDS IS PART JOY AND PART GUERRILLA WARFARE**

ED ASNER

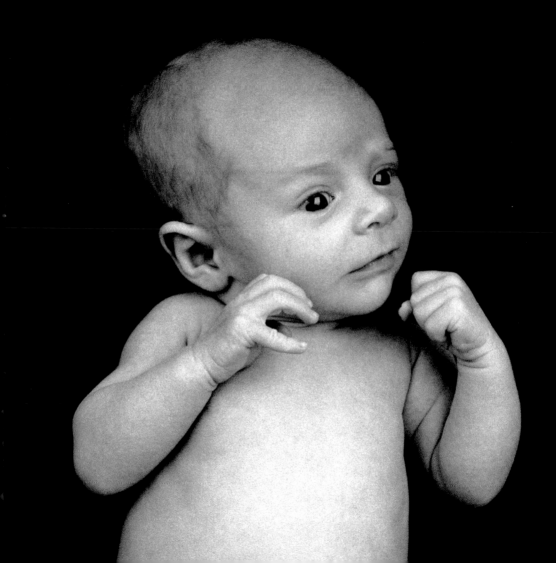

**"**

## HAVING A FAMILY

### IS LIKE HAVING A BOWLING ALLEY INSTALLED IN YOUR BRAIN.

**"**

MARTIN MULL

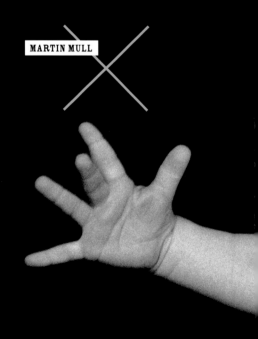

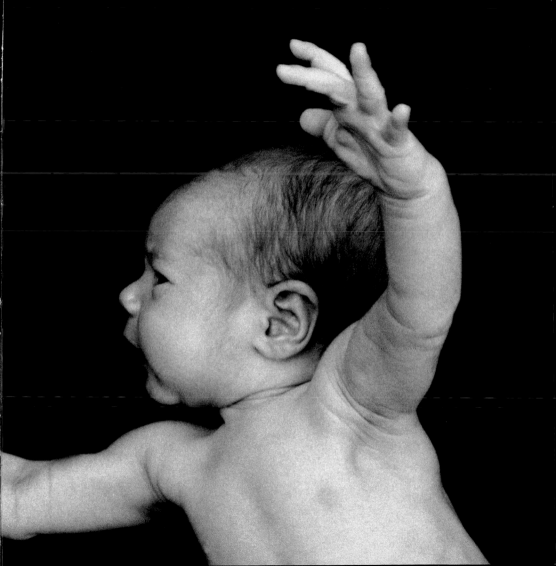

66

A BABY IS KIND OF LIKE HAVING A BLENDER, BUT YOU DON'T HAVE A TOP FOR IT.

99

JERRY SEINFELD

"

LIFE DOESN'T COME WITH AN INSTRUCTION BOOK – THAT'S WHY WE HAVE FATHERS.

"

H JACKSON BROWN SR.

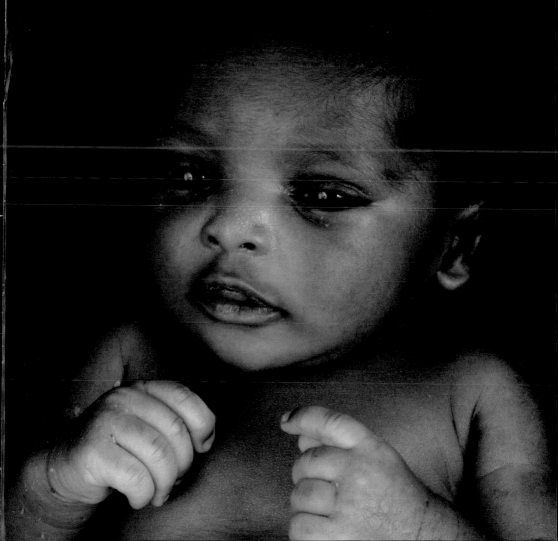

"

SOMETIMES THE POOREST MAN

LEAVES HIS CHILDREN

THE RICHEST INHERITANCE

"

RUTH E RENKEL

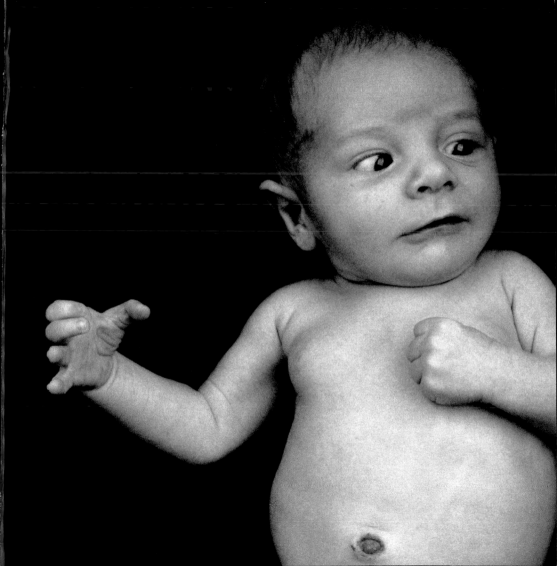

**" ONE FATHER IS MORE THAN A HUNDRED SCHOOLMASTERS "**

ENGLISH PROVERB

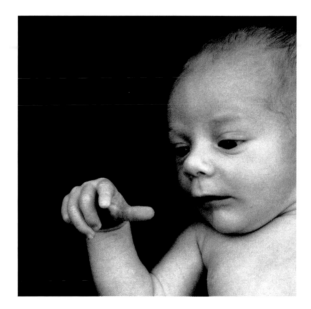

"ALWAYS **KISS** YOUR CHILDREN GOODNIGHT -EVEN IF THEY ARE ALREADY *asleep*"

H.JACKSON BROWN JR.